THE USA

The United States chooses a new president – and the world watches. On one terrible day 3,000 people die in New York – and the world watches. To millions of people, the United States is one of the most interesting countries in the world.

There are American things around us all the time – food, music, books, and films. But what *is* the United States, and how did it become the country it is today? Why did it go to war against Britain – and then against itself? What is life like in America today – and what does it mean to be an American? Come and find out about America's history, its government, its people, music, food, cities and its wild places – and get a little closer to the real United States.

T0347121

OXFORD BOOKWORMS LIBRARY

Factfiles

The USA

Stage 3 (1000 headwords)

Factfiles Series Editor: Christine Lindop

For Rae

ALISON BAXTER

The USA

OXFORD UNIVERSITY PRESS

OXFORD
UNIVERSITY PRESS

ISBN: 978 0 19 423391 0   Book
ISBN: 978 0 19 462104 5   Book and audio pack

Printed by Ashford Colour Ltd

Word count (main text): 10,188

For more information on the Oxford Bookworms Library,
visit www.oup.com/elt/gradedreaders

ACKNOWLEDGEMENTS

Alamy Stock Photo pp.2 (Pocahontas/North Wind Picture Archives), 16 (Zuni Indian jewellery/
Robert Harding Picture Library Ltd.), 21 (Harriet Tubman/The Print Collector), 21 (Frederick
Douglass/Michael Ventura), 24 (Capitol Building, Washington DC/Phil Degginger), 26 (The
White House/JLImages), 33 (baseball match/Paul Quayle), 35 (American burger/Brent Hofacker),
47 (Paramount studios/Paul Briden), 56 (surfer/David Fleetham); Bridgeman Art Library Ltd
p.28 (*Summertime*, 1943 (oil on canvas), Hopper, Edward (1882–1967)/Delaware Art Museum,
Wilmington, USA); Getty Images pp.3 (The First Thanksgiving/Barney Burstein), 6 (Declaration
of Independence/Bettmann), 8 (US Capitol building/Richard T. Nowitz), 9 (cotton picking/
Bettmann), 11 (General Sherman/Bettmann), 12 (Deputy John Fletcher/Bettmann), 14 (bison
hunting/Robert Holmes), 17 (arriving in New York/Archive Holdings Inc.), 19 (San Francisco/
Gary Cralle), 22 (segregation/Bettmann), 23 (Martin Luther King/Bettmann), 25 (congress/Chip
Somodevilla), 29 (suburbs/Alan Schein Photography), 31 (shopping mall/Owen Franken), 35 (fast
food sign/Ionas Kaltenbach), 37 (Louis Armstrong/David Redferns), 39 (Snoop Dogg/Ethan Miller),
41 (Boston/Hubert Stadler), 42 (Asendorf house/Philippa Lewis/Arcaid Images), 45 (redwood
trees/Ken Biggs), 46 (cable car/John Lamb), 51 (Grand Canyon Skywalk/Photo by Mike Kline
(notkalvin)), 52 (Niagara Falls/Cheryl Forbes), 53 (Simon Lake/Don Johnston), 55 (Aurora Borealis/
Daniel J Cox); Oxford University Press pp.viii (Waikiki Beach/Photodisc), 1 (Death Valley/Digital
Vision), 4 (pumpkin pie/Purestock), 44 (Las Vegas/Photodisc), 44 (Mount Rushmore/Photodisc),
44 (Golden Gate Bridge/Photodisc), 44 (Statue of Liberty/Photodisc), 44 (Grand Canyon/Corel),
44 (Hawaii/Photodisc), 49 (mountain top/Photodisc); Rex Shutterstock p.36 (John Lee Hooker/
Everett Collection); Reuters News Agency, Thomson Reuters p.44 (Viva Las Vegas/Steve Marcus).

Cover: Getty Images (Mount Rushmore/VisionsofAmerica/Joe Sohm)

CONTENTS

Death Valley, California

1 In the beginning

Think of a big, beautiful, empty land with mountains, forests, lakes, animals, and fish, but no people. This was America 16,000 years ago. Around that time, the first people probably arrived in Alaska from Asia. They travelled south and became the Native Americans of North America and the Maya, Aztecs, Inca and other peoples of Central and South America. The Inuit (Eskimos) came to Canada and the Arctic the same way. But there are only a few of these peoples in America today.

In the sixteenth century Europeans started to come to America, and soon after that, they brought slaves from Africa to work for them. Large numbers of immigrants continued to arrive from all over the world until the middle of the twentieth century. The empty land was now full of people, speaking different languages and with different ideas. There are just three countries now in North America – Canada, Mexico and the USA – but there were nearly several more. And the 300 million people who live in the fifty states of the United States are not all the same. About 67 per cent are white, 13 per cent Hispanic (Spanish-speaking), 13 per cent black, 4 per cent Asian and just 1 per cent Native American. Most of them speak English, but it is not the same English as people speak in Britain, and many Americans speak Spanish as their first language.

So how was the USA born? How did it grow? What kind of country is it now? This book will try to answer those questions, and many more.

2 The Pilgrim Fathers

The name 'America' comes from an Italian businessman called Amerigo Vespucci, who sailed to South America between 1499 and 1502. But he was not the first European to make the dangerous journey across the Atlantic. The Vikings came to 'Vinland' (probably Canada or New England) from Scandinavia around AD 1000, but they did not stay. Then, in 1492, a brave Italian sailor called Christopher Columbus reached the Caribbean while he was looking for a sea route from Europe to India. Columbus called the Native Americans 'Indians' because he thought that he had reached India. When Columbus returned to Europe he told people about his adventures and other sailors like Cabot and Cartier followed him across the Atlantic. Europeans came to fish the rich seas of America too.

But it was only in the seventeenth century that the French, the Dutch and the British all came to live in North America: the French in Quebec, the Dutch in New York and the British in Virginia and New England. Two very different groups of English people crossed the Atlantic. The first group began the colony of Jamestown in Virginia in

Pocahontas with her son

1607. They hoped to find gold there, but life was very hard for them. There was very little food, and many of them died during the first winter. Then Pocahontas, the daughter of a Native American chief, became a friend of Captain John Smith and helped him and the other English people. She later married a man called John Rolfe and went to England with him. Luckily, tobacco saved the young colony. It was easy to grow tobacco in Virginia, and smoking was becoming very fashionable. People in the colony stopped looking for gold and began to grow tobacco, which they sold in Europe. Soon they started to bring people from Africa to work as their slaves and help them to grow more and more.

John Smith travelled north in 1614 to the part of America that he called New England. When he returned to London, he told people that it was a good place to live. In 1620, another group of 101 English men, women and children arrived in Plymouth, Massachusetts. These people are called the 'Pilgrims' or 'Pilgrim Fathers', and they had very strong ideas about religion. They did not want to live in England because they did not agree with the English church, so they sailed to America in a ship called the *Mayflower*. They farmed the land and they bought and sold animal skins. They thought that all people were equal and so they did not have slaves.

The Pilgrims too were often ill and hungry, and nearly half of them died in the first year. But they had help from some of the Native Americans, particularly a man called Squanto. He went to Europe as a prisoner in 1605, and spent some years in England, so he spoke some English. He showed the Pilgrims how to hunt and grow corn.

In the autumn of 1621, the Pilgrims had a big dinner to give thanks for the first food that they had grown themselves. This day was called Thanksgiving, and Americans still celebrate it every year, on the fourth Thursday of November. It is one of the most important holidays in the year, and people often travel many hundreds of kilometres to be with their families. They eat a big dinner with two of the foods that the Pilgrim Fathers found in America, turkey and pie filled with pumpkin.

Pumpkin pie

3

The War of Independence

More and more British people came to live on the east coast of North America in the seventeenth century, starting colonies in Maryland, Rhode Island, Connecticut, New Hampshire, North and South Carolina, New Jersey, and Pennsylvania. Georgia followed in the eighteenth century, when the British also took New York and Delaware from the Dutch. By 1770, there were thirteen colonies along the east coast of North America, and they were all governed by Britain. But Britain was a long way away, and the people of the colonies became angry at the high taxes that the government made them pay. In December 1773 a group of men threw 342 boxes of tea into the sea at Boston because they did not want to pay the British tax on it. This was the 'Boston Tea Party'.

The British government was now angry too, and in April 1775 some Americans fought a group of British soldiers at the towns of Lexington and Concord, near Boston in Massachusetts. More and more Americans arrived until the British soldiers had to move back to Boston. A few months later, after the Battle of Bunker Hill, near Boston, it was clear that Britain was at war with its American colonies.

A rich farmer from Virginia, George Washington, became the chief of the American army. People tell a story about Washington, to show that he was an honest man. They say that when he was a boy he cut down a tree and this made his father angry. But when his father asked him about it, he told him, 'I cannot tell a lie, I cut down the tree.'

The colonies did not say that they wanted to be fully independent until the summer of 1776. A man called Thomas Jefferson wrote the famous 'Declaration of Independence' where he said that the king, George the Third, was not a good king because he had not let his people have their rights: the right to life, to freedom and to happiness. The day of the Declaration of Independence, 4 July, is another important American holiday.

The Americans finally won the war in October 1781, and two years after that, they were free to govern themselves. In 1789 they made George Washington their first president. Although he wanted to go back to his farm at Mount Vernon and enjoy a quiet life he stayed president until 1797. He died in 1799, just two years after he returned home.

The names 'United States of America' and 'American' were first used at the time of the War of Independence. The thirteen colonies became the first thirteen states of the United States. In 1803, after Jefferson became the third president, he bought a large area of land in the Midwest from France. It was five times as big as France, and it only cost 15 million dollars. Jefferson then sent two brave men, Meriwether Lewis and William Clark, to travel across America all the way to the Pacific. With a young Native American woman called Sacagawea to help them, the two

Signing the Declaration of Independence

men travelled 13,000 kilometres between 1804 and 1806. They found many animals, plants, and fish that were new to Europeans, and they made maps of the rivers, mountains, and land that they crossed.

In 1819, the USA bought Florida from Spain. The United States was now twice as big as it had been in 1781. And by 1848, after it won Texas and the Southwest from Mexico, it had grown again. It now reached all the way from the Atlantic to the Pacific, over 5,000 kilometres.

Finally, the American government bought the land northwest of Canada from Russia in 1867 for 7.2 million dollars and it became the state of Alaska in 1959. The American flag, known as the 'Stars and Stripes', first appeared at the time of the War of Independence. It has a stripe for each of the first thirteen states, and a star was added every time a new state joined, so there are now fifty stars. The last star was added when the beautiful islands of Hawaii, in the Pacific 4,000 kilometres west of California, became the fiftieth state of the USA in 1959.

The 'Stars and Stripes'

4   The Civil War

The young country grew quickly, and by the middle of the nineteenth century it had 31 million people. But there were serious differences between the North and the South. And in 1861 a terrible war started. At least 600,000 people died in the battles or from disease.

The war began because the southern states kept slaves to work in the cotton fields but slaves were not allowed in the North. People from the South wanted to have slaves in the new lands of the west, but people from the North argued against this. In 1860, Abraham Lincoln was elected sixteenth president of the USA. He belonged to the Republican Party,

Slaves picking cotton

which did not want people to have slaves. On 24 December, South Carolina said that it wanted to be independent and the other southern states soon followed. The fighting began on 12 April 1861, at Fort Sumter.

The South had some of the best soldiers – one was the famous Robert E. Lee – and they had plenty of money from selling their cotton to Britain. But the North had more men and more factories. They also had Lincoln, one of the best presidents that the USA has ever had. He was born on a farm in Kentucky but he worked hard in order to learn as much as he could. Lincoln made the Republican Party strong and spoke about rights and freedom. A very important battle was won by the soldiers of the North at Gettysburg in Pennsylvania in 1863. Lincoln spoke there afterwards about the brave soldiers who had died. This became known as the Gettysburg Address and contains the famous words: '. . . government of the people, by the people, for the people.'

Two famous soldiers helped the North to win the war. General Sherman is remembered in a famous song that tells the story of how he took 60,000 of his soldiers on a journey of 400 kilometres from Atlanta in Georgia to the Atlantic coast. In this way he cut a wide path through the southern states, and after that it was hard for the armies of the South to join together and fight the North. After the war, Sherman became head of the American army. General Ulysses S. Grant represented the North at Appomattox in 1865 when the South, under Lee, accepted that they had lost the war. Grant was very fair to Lee's soldiers, who did not have to go

to prison. Some years later, in 1868, he became president.

Sadly, on 14 April 1865, five days after the end of the war, President Lincoln was shot at the theatre by a man called John Wilkes Booth, who hated Lincoln and was angry about the war. After Lincoln's death, the new president was not strong enough to bring the North and the South together, and people continued to argue about the rights of black people.

During the Civil War Louisa May Alcott wrote her famous book *Little Women* about a family of four girls living at home in the North with their mother while their father was away at the war. Another very famous book (and later film) about the war is *Gone with the Wind* written in 1936. It tells the story of Scarlett O'Hara, a rich young girl who is living comfortably in the southern state of Georgia when her life is destroyed by the war.

General Sherman in Georgia

5 The Wild West

During the nineteenth century, more and more people went to live in the West of the USA. The 'Wild West' that you can see on television and in films is full of cowboys, Indians, and fighting. In fact there were very few cowboys – no more than 40,000 – and real cowboys did not shoot each other or fight Indians very often. They worked hard at their job, taking

A cowboy in the nineteenth century

care of the cows, and at least a quarter of them were black or Mexican. They took cows from Texas up to the railway towns in Kansas and Missouri. From there the cows were sent to Chicago and killed, and the meat was sent to the East and sold.

The cowboys almost disappeared after about thirty years because the government gave the land to farmers and their families. From 1862 to 1900 more than half a million farmers came to live in the West, where they made new farms and grew food. One family that moved west was the Ingalls family, whose daughter Laura Ingalls Wilder told the story

of their journey in books like *Little House on the Prairie*. Life for these farmers was very hard, particularly in winter. The farms were very lonely, but soon the railways helped to bring people together. In 1869, the railway line from the east met the line from the west in Utah, so then Americans could travel right across the USA by train.

Before the railway, from 1860 to 1861 the post was carried across the country by the famous Pony Express. Horses and riders waited at different places; one man rode with a bag of letters for about 120 kilometres and then gave it to the next man. In this way, letters only took about ten days to cross the country. One very well-known rider was Buffalo Bill Cody. He later became a soldier and a hunter – they say that he shot 4,280 buffalo in one year! In the 1880s, Buffalo Bill started his Wild West Show, a kind of travelling theatre, with the famous cowgirl Annie Oakley.

6 Native Americans

There were about two million Native Americans in North America in the fifteenth century when the Europeans arrived. They belonged to 300 different groups and spoke more than 2,000 different languages. Sadly, the Europeans fought and killed many Native Americans and also brought diseases which killed them. The film *The Last of the Mohicans*, from the book by James Fenimore Cooper, shows the sad end of a group of Native Americans in the eighteenth century.

The Native Americans that we know as 'Indians' in cowboy films lived in the West. They were the Cheyenne, the Blackfoot, and the Sioux (also known as Lakota), for example.

Native Americans hunting buffalo

There were about 60 million buffalo in North America, and the Native Americans hunted them and used them for food, clothes, houses, knives, and other things. But when the Europeans arrived, they wanted to take the land for farms or railways. They shot millions of buffalo, and by 1900 there were fewer than a thousand of these animals in all of the USA – and fewer than 250,000 Native Americans!

The great Sioux chief Sitting Bull fought against the white men who wanted to move his people from their own land to 'Indian' land further west. He won an important battle at Little Big Horn in 1876 but could not win the war. The 'Indian wars' ended in 1890 with the Battle of Wounded Knee, when American soldiers killed many Sioux men, women and children. After this, Native Americans had to live in special places called 'reservations'.

Even today, about a third of the 4.4 million Native Americans live on reservations. They are often very poor and a lot of them do not have jobs, so they sometimes drink too much alcohol in order to forget their problems. Some Native Americans build casinos where people can go to win money from cards and other games, and this brings in money for the reservations. Other groups refuse to do this and also do not allow alcohol on their reservations.

Many of the big reservations are in the Southwest, the home of a different type of Native American. Among the people of the Southwest are the Hopi and the Zuni. They keep sheep, make pots, and also make beautiful jewellery from silver and blue-green stones. Their religion is very important to them; their dancing often has a religious meaning, and they make beautiful religious pictures.

The biggest reservation, where 200,000 Navajo people live, is nearly 65,000 square kilometres. The Navajo make wonderful coloured blankets. The Navajo language is very unusual; during the Second World War, the American army used Navajo soldiers to send secret radio messages that the enemy could not understand.

Native American jewellery

7   New Americans

At the beginning of the nineteenth century most American families had come from Britain, Germany and Scandinavia, and they were farmers or businesspeople. But soon that began to change. Factories were built and cities grew; poor people arrived from other countries, hoping to find work. Between 1840 and 1900, about five million people came from one country – Ireland. Another five million immigrants came from Italy, and millions more from Russia, Poland, and other countries of Eastern Europe, hoping to find jobs and freedom. America kept an 'open door' until 1924 and about 27 million people arrived between 1880 and 1930. They were often poor, had different religions, and had not been to school for very long; there was a lot of prejudice against them.

Immigrants arriving in New York by ship

Immigrants from Europe arrived at Ellis Island in New York, where they were all checked for disease and for other problems. Close to Ellis Island is the Statue of Liberty (liberty means 'freedom'). On it are these famous words: 'Give me your tired, your poor . . .' The statue welcomed the poor, tired immigrants who hoped for a happier life in the USA.

The Chinese immigrants who arrived in the West of the USA also found prejudice. Many people came to live in California after gold was found there in 1848, and among them were 300,000 Chinese. Many of the Chinese stayed to work building the new railways. Like black people and Native Americans, the Chinese had no civil rights and after 1882, they were no longer allowed to enter the USA. But in the twentieth century Chinese people started to arrive again and now the cities of the west coast have large numbers of Chinese families. The writer Amy Tan tells stories about life as a Chinese American in *The Joy Luck Club* and other books.

Today, most immigrants to the USA come from Spanish-speaking countries like Mexico and Puerto Rico. More than six million have arrived since 1980 and Spanish has become the second language of the United States.

The Irish, Italians and Eastern Europeans usually stayed in the big cities of the East or the Midwest, like New York, Boston or Chicago, and worked in the factories. Although most of them learned English and became Americans, they also wanted to keep their own way of life. So in many cities you can find places called Little Italy or Chinatown, for example, where the restaurants have Italian or Chinese food. In New York, Boston, and Chicago, St Patrick's Day is a big celebration for the Irish on 17 March and Chinese New Year is a big celebration in San Francisco.

Chinatown, San Francisco

8 Black Americans

Today about 39 million of the 300 million people in the USA are black. They used to live mostly in the South, working in the cotton and tobacco fields. A story about the hard life of slaves, *Uncle Tom's Cabin* by Harriet Beecher Stowe, was very popular in the mid-nineteenth century. It made a lot of people see that keeping slaves was wrong, and it told the exciting story of how a slave family escaped, using the 'Underground Railway'. This was not a real railway but a number of places where slaves could find help. People in each house could show them the way to the next safe house.

Harriet Tubman and Frederick Douglass were famous slaves who helped many other slaves to escape from the South to the North using the Underground Railway. Frederick Douglass escaped in 1838 and started to work for the freedom of other black people. He had understood that in order to be free he needed to learn to read and write and he wrote a book about his life. After this he travelled to Europe to speak about slavery and later returned to New York and started several newspapers. During the Civil War he told black men to join the army to fight for the North and after the war he worked for the government.

Harriet Tubman travelled 140 kilometres to freedom in 1849 with the help of white people and free blacks. Although it was dangerous, she returned in order to help her family, and she bravely said, 'I can only die once.' In the 1850s she helped more than 300 slaves escape.

After the Civil War, white southerners were angry that

Harriet Tubman

Frederick Douglass

they had lost the war and angry that slaves were now free. They showed a lot of prejudice against black people. Some white people joined the Ku Klux Klan, groups of men who dressed in white, covered their faces, and went out to beat and murder black people. Black men could not vote until 1870, and even after they got the right to vote, they often did not use it because they were frightened. The book *To Kill a Mocking Bird* by Harper Lee tells the frightening story of a black man, Tom Robinson, in 1930s Alabama. Although Tom has done nothing wrong, people easily believe that he is a criminal – just because he is black.

In the twentieth century, black people began to travel to the cities of the North to look for work, so there are now more black people in the North than in the South. But even in the North, they lived separately. In the South they had to sit separately on buses and eat in separate parts of restaurants. Until 1954, they also had to go to different schools.

Then in the 1950s, a churchman called Martin Luther King began to fight for the civil rights of black people. Groups of black people started to break the law, but not in a violent way. In 1955 in Montgomery, Alabama, a woman called Rosa Parks became famous when she refused to give her seat on a bus to a white man. Then more black people refused to use the buses, and the bus companies lost a lot of money. Black people also started to go into 'whites only' restaurants.

In August 1963 200,000 people met in Washington and heard Martin Luther King speak about the need for black people to be equal with white people. He began with these words, which have become famous: 'I have a dream . . .' Finally, in 1964, a law was passed which gave black people their rights and Martin Luther King was given the Nobel Peace Prize. But in 1968, he was murdered in Memphis and fighting started in more than a hundred cities.

During the 1970s and 1980s, prejudice against black people slowly began to appear less often, and many black people now have good jobs in business and government. A black woman like Condoleezza Rice can represent the American government in other countries and perhaps even think about becoming president. But there are still problems. When Hurricane Katrina destroyed the city of New Orleans in 2005, most of the people who lost their houses were black. Many of them waited a long time for help from the government. Was it because they were black? A lot of people think so.

Martin Luther King

9   The government of the USA

The government of the USA has three separate but equal parts: Congress, the President, and the Supreme Court. Women got the vote in 1920 and all Americans can now vote when they are eighteen. There are some rights that all Americans have by law: for example, the right to speak freely.

Congress makes the laws. There are in fact two 'houses' of Congress: the Senate and the House of Representatives.

The Capitol Building, Washington DC

Congress

There are a hundred people in the Senate (two from each state) and they are elected for six years. There are 435 people in the House of Representatives, and they are elected for two years only. The states with more people, like California, have more representatives. States which do not have many people, like Wyoming or Delaware, only have one representative. The President is elected by votes from each state. A state has the same number of votes as the number of its representatives and senators, so the states with most people become very important. Florida has 25 votes and so when just 51 per cent of people in Florida voted for George Bush in 2000 he got all 25 votes from that state.

The President is the most important of all the people in the government. He (until now the president has always been a man) is the chief of the country, like a king or queen, and he is also the head of the army. He is elected for four years and no one can be president for more than eight years. He can say 'no' to laws passed by Congress (but Congress can

The White House

also say 'no' to him), and he chooses the judges for the Supreme Court. He lives and works in the White House in Washington DC.

The Supreme Court is the most important court in the country and has nine judges; their job is to decide what the laws mean. They can also say that Congress has made a law which is wrong, or that the President has done something wrong.

As well as the government in Washington, each state has its own government. Laws can be very different from one state to the next. They say very different things about, for example, how old you must be to get married, or to drive a car. Different states punish criminals differently too; in some states, you must die if you murder someone, but in others you only go to prison. The island of Puerto Rico in the Caribbean is not a state, but it is not independent either. People from Puerto Rico do not pay American taxes and cannot vote in American elections.

There are two important political parties: the Republicans and the Democrats. The Republicans want people to work to help themselves, and so they think that taxes should be low. The Democrats think that the government should help the poor and so it needs taxes. But the difference between the two is not always clear. After the 2000 election a map showed that the Democrat states were on the north-east and west coasts and around the Great Lakes in the North, but the Republican states were across the centre and in the South of the USA.

Americans are happy that they do not have a king or queen and they say that anyone can become president. But you need a lot of money to tell people about yourself and your ideas, so it is easier to become president if you come from a rich family. The second and sixth presidents, John Adams and John Quincy Adams, were father and son, and in modern times the Bush family has had two presidents. From 1989 to 1993 George Bush was president, and in 2001 his son George W. Bush became president too. At the same time Jeb Bush, the brother of George W. Bush, was head of the government of Florida. Some other families have also nearly had two presidents. President Kennedy's brother Robert hoped to become president but he was killed in 1968, and many people think that Hillary Clinton will follow her husband Bill. If she does, she will be the first woman president.

A president must also be able to speak well to crowds of people. Ronald Reagan, the fortieth president, could do this because he used to be an actor. He became head of the government of California in 1967, and was president from 1981 to 1989. Another actor, Arnold Schwarzenegger, also became head of the government of California in 2003 and some people believe that film stars will become successful politicians more often in future.

10   Living in the USA

Many people who have never been to the USA recognize it from films and TV programmes. Then there is the work of the artist Edward Hopper, whose pictures of ordinary American people, streets, and houses, in the city and in the country, make us think of old films. But what is life in America really like?

Most Americans who have jobs live more comfortably than people in almost any other country in the world. They usually work a forty-hour week and they have two weeks' holiday a year as well as holidays like Thanksgiving and Christmas. In 60 per cent of families, the husband and the wife both work. Although more than 40 per cent of the land is farmed, not many people work as farmers, and fewer Americans work in factories than in the past. Most jobs are

An American family

now in places like hospitals, banks, hotels, and shops. If you do not have a job (and around 6 per cent of Americans do not), life is hard. The government gives you a little money but it is not enough to buy everything that you need. How many Americans are poor? Around 13 per cent of all Americans are poor, but 25 per cent of black people and 22 per cent of Hispanic people are poor.

The money in the USA is the dollar, which contains a hundred cents. Some coins have special names: 5 cents is a nickel, 10 cents is a dime, and 25 cents is a quarter. In taxis, restaurants, and other places people give a 'tip' – extra money on top of the price. Without this extra money, many workers do not have enough money to live.

Americans do not use kilograms and kilometres but pounds and miles. Dates are also written differently from dates in Britain: 4 July is 7/4, not 4/7. Sadly, the world learned about how Americans say dates on 11 September 2001, the date that we remember as 'nine eleven'.

Because the USA is such a big country, the time changes as you travel from one side to the other. When it is 12 midday in New York (Eastern Time), it is 11 a.m. in Kansas (Central Time), 10 a.m. in Arizona (Mountain Time), and 9 a.m. in Seattle (Pacific Time). And the time in Alaska is 8 a.m. and in Hawaii 7 a.m.

The pictures by the artist Norman Rockwell tell stories of the life of ordinary families from the 1920s to the 1970s. Although they are often too happy to be true, they give us an idea of life in small towns that has not all disappeared yet. Two-thirds of Americans own their homes, often with a garden. At least 85 per cent of families have a car and more than 75 per cent of Americans drive to work. They also use their car to go to 'drive-in' restaurants, coffee shops, or even banks. Henry Ford, who made the famous Ford cars, was born in Michigan, near Detroit. His 'Model T' (1908) was the first car that was cheap enough for ordinary people. 'Anyone can drive a Ford,' they said, and by 1918 half the cars in the USA were Model Ts. Now more and more Americans drive very big cars called SUVs.

The USA does not have a state religion, and no religion is allowed in schools. Instead every morning American students make a promise to the American flag. But over 80 per cent of Americans belong to a Christian church and Christianity is very important, particularly in the South of the USA. In some states books are not allowed in schools if they say something different from the Christian story of the beginning of the world. Some churches are just for black people and black churchmen like Martin Luther King and

Jesse Jackson have worked very hard for the rights of black people. One large religious group is the Latter Day Saints, or Mormons, who live mainly in Utah. They have very strong ideas about how to dress and are against alcohol and tobacco.

If they do not want to go out, Americans can stay at home and watch television. Nearly all families have a TV and an ordinary family watches more than seven hours a day. There are over 10,000 TV stations, and most of them belong to businesses, not to the government. American TV programmes are sold all over the world. There are more than 1,500 daily newspapers but most of them are just for one city. The most popular newspaper is *USA Today,* which sells five million copies a day. You can buy papers like the *New York Times* and the *Washington Post* everywhere, as well as the magazines *Time* and *Newsweek.*

An American shopping centre

And, of course, Americans love to shop; the supermarket first appeared in America, and now many shops are open twenty-four hours a day. Some of the biggest shopping centres in the world are in the USA – Mall of America in Minneapolis has over 500 shops and covers 1.25 million square metres. You could put thirty-two Boeing 747 planes into it!

Americans have to pay if they visit a doctor or go to hospital, but they do not usually pay to go to school. Schools, like the laws, are different from state to state, but in most places, everyone goes to school for about twelve years. The years are called 'grades': grades 1 to 5 are 'elementary school', 6 to 8 are 'middle school', and 9 to 12 'high school'. About 85 per cent of students finish high school and celebrate with a party known as a 'prom'. They also make a 'year book'; this has photos of all the students in their class and some information about each person. Films like *American Graffiti* and *The Breakfast Club* have shown what life is like at an American high school. About half the students who finish high school go on to study for another two or four years. Harvard and Yale in the east and Berkeley in California are among America's famous universities.

Most Americans enjoy sports, and baseball, basketball, and football are popular. American football is a very different game from European football; players carry the ball more than they use their feet. But the favourite sport in the USA is baseball. The film *Field of Dreams* tells the story of a farmer from Iowa in the mid-west, played by Kevin Costner, who dreams of the Chicago White Sox team and makes a baseball field for them in a field on his farm. Baseball is played by two teams of nine people. Each player from the first team tries to hit the ball and run round a big square from corner to corner. The players from the second team try to catch the ball. Players try to get all the way round the square before the other team can get the ball to a corner. After three players go 'out', it is the turn of the second team to hit the ball. Some famous teams are the Los Angeles Dodgers, the New York Yankees, and the Boston Red Sox. Perhaps the greatest baseball player in history was Babe Ruth. He was born in 1895 and played with the Boston Red Sox and then the New York Yankees. He died in 1948 but he is still remembered today.

Baseball, America's favourite sport

11 Eating and drinking the American way

What do Americans eat? American 'fast food' is sold in restaurants in almost every country of the world. The most famous examples are probably hamburgers, hot dogs, and chips, which are called 'french fries'. A lot of Americans are fat, perhaps because they eat too much fast food. These days many families in America do not sit down to eat dinner together but eat alone every few hours all through the day. Sweet foods, like pies and ice-cream, are very popular too. The famous Ben and Jerry's ice-cream started in Vermont in New England. But more and more people are interested in healthy eating, so they choose foods that are better for them or they decide to stop eating meat.

If you visit the USA you will be able to enjoy an American breakfast. Eggs are cooked in a lot of different ways; 'sunny side up' means with the yellow on top, 'over easy' means with the yellow underneath but still soft. With your breakfast you can drink as much coffee as you want, all for the same price. In fact, you can drink coffee all day in the USA. It is of course the home of Starbucks, which since the 1990s has changed the way everybody drinks coffee. Now all over the world you can go to a coffee shop and choose from a very long menu of coffees.

What else can you drink that is really American? Coca-Cola was first made in 1886 by an American called John Pemberton. Today it is sold in 195 countries and Coke™ is one of the best-known words in the world. You can also find excellent American wine from the west coast, particularly California. But Americans are not allowed to buy alcohol until they are 21. In many states you cannot smoke in places like bars, restaurants, and places of work. From 1920 to 1933, during Prohibition, it was against the law to drink alcohol at all in the USA, but many people still wanted to drink it. So criminals like Al Capone brought alcohol into the country and made a lot of money.

In American restaurants you can eat all kinds of tasty food from different countries: Chinese, Mexican, and Italian, for example. The immigrants who came to the USA brought their own favourite foods with them. These then changed into new styles of cooking that are special to the USA. For example Tex Mex (Texan Mexican) food is like Mexican but uses more meat. Cajun food is spicy food from Louisiana with unusual names like 'gumbo' and 'jambalaya'. 'Soul food' is the food that black families like to cook in the South. It is usually meat or fish with green vegetables, sweet potatoes, and corn bread, perhaps with pie afterwards.

A hamburger

12 Music from America

All over the world people listen to American music. It began with the songs of black American slaves. Black slaves in the South sang work songs and religious songs with a shape of 'call and response'. This is like a conversation in music – one person sings, and then another answers. When the slaves got their freedom after the Civil War they began to tell their own stories in music called the 'blues', particularly in the area around the Mississippi River. It had the same shape, where the singer sings and the guitar answers. The word 'blue' can mean sad, and the songs tell a sad story of hard work and danger.

John Lee Hooker

Oxford Bookworms Library

Audio Download
Stage 3
The USA

To download the audio for this title

1 Go to www.oup.com/elt/download

2 Use this code and your email address

Your download code

OXFORD

UNIVERSITY PRESS

ISBN 978-0-19-462210-3

9 780194 622103

At the beginning of the twentieth century black people moved from the South to the North to find work. They took their music with them to cities like Chicago and Detroit. Musicians like Muddy Waters, Willie Dixon, John Lee Hooker, and Howlin' Wolf were the first to use electric guitars. Records of the blues became very popular in the 1920s and 1930s when singers like Bessie Smith became famous. In the 1950s Elvis Presley, who came from Mississippi, was the first white singer to sing music that came from the blues. In the 1960s 'soul' was born from the old style blues, with singers like Marvin Gaye and Otis Redding. The city of Detroit has a lot of motor (car) factories, and it gave the name 'Motown' (motor town) to soul music. People all over the world listened to Motown singers like Diana Ross, Stevie Wonder, and the Jackson Five in the 1960s and 70s.

Jazz was born in the city of New Orleans, on the Mississippi River in the far south of the USA. It too probably began with the songs and dancing of black slaves in the

Louis Armstrong

1830s. The musician Jelly Roll Morton said he was the first to play 'jazz' in 1897, but nobody really knows when it began. Black musicians like Louis Armstrong became famous in the 1920s in Chicago, and jazz music became popular across the world after it travelled to New York and Paris in the 1930s. George Gershwin, who made music for films and theatre, thought jazz was an important part of American life and he used it in music like his *Rhapsody in Blue*. During the Second World War, American soldiers brought the 'swing' music of the big dance bands like Glenn Miller to Europe. This was not jazz but part of the same family of music.

Now names of great jazz musicians like Miles Davis, Stan Getz, and John Coltrane are known all over the world, and people write, sing, and play jazz in many countries. But New Orleans, where it all began, is not the exciting place that it once was. The city was famous for Mardi Gras, which was like a wonderful party in the streets, with colorful clothes, music, and dancing. But the city is on land which is lower than the sea, and in 2005 Hurricane Katrina covered its streets and houses with water. Several thousand people died, and the city was badly damaged. Will New Orleans live again one day as the home of music? The musicians hope so, and many still come every year to play in the New Orleans Jazz Festival.

Another popular kind of American music is 'country' (or 'country and western') which has its home in Nashville, Tennessee. It started from the music of the Scottish, Irish, and English people who came to live in the Appalachian Mountains. Country music began to be really popular in the 1920s, when Jimmie Rodgers and the Carter family made the first country records and the Grand Ole Opry

Snoop Dogg

radio show started in Nashville. Music is still recorded in Nashville and if you go there you can visit the Country Music 'Hall of Fame'. One of the most famous women country singers is Dolly Parton, who has also appeared in films like *9 to 5* and *Steel Magnolias*. Johnny Cash, 'The Man in Black', sold millions of records in the 1960s and 1970s, and was still popular when he died in 2003. The 2005 film *Walk the Line*, which told the story of Johnny's early life, was very successful.

In the 1990s a new kind of music called 'rap' became popular in New York. It came from black and Puerto Rican people and told of a dangerous life on the streets, where there was fighting and killing. Rappers don't sing but they talk very fast over music. Some famous rappers are Eminem, Snoop Dogg, and Missy Elliott.

13 Some great American cities

Some of America's greatest cities are on the Atlantic coast. Boston in the Northeast, where the fight for independence began in the eighteenth century, is one of the oldest cities in the USA. Here you can walk the 'Freedom Trail' and visit the place where the tea was thrown into the sea. A few kilometres away in the city of Cambridge is Harvard, the oldest university in the USA, which was opened in 1636. The famous Massachusetts Institute of Technology (MIT) is in Cambridge too.

Perhaps the most famous family in twentieth-century Boston was the Kennedy family. Like many other Boston families, they came from Ireland. They became very rich, and John F. Kennedy, a Democrat, became President of the United States in 1961. At that time he said '. . . ask not what your country can do for you, but what you can do for your country.' He and his beautiful wife Jacqueline were young and popular, but sadly, in 1963, Kennedy was shot and killed in Dallas, Texas.

New York is the biggest city in the USA. It is a great place for theatre, shopping and restaurants. It is also the home of the United Nations, whose offices are in a beautiful glass skyscraper. But people remember two even taller skyscrapers, those of the World Trade Center, because on

The city of Boston

11 September 2001 two planes flew into them and killed nearly 3,000 people.

The Empire State Building is now the most famous skyscraper in the city once again. It is 443 metres high, has 102 floors, and has appeared in *King Kong* and many other films. The Statue of Liberty is another favourite place for tourists. It is 93 metres tall and the best way to see it is by boat. It was a present from the people of France for the hundredth birthday of the USA in 1876.

Many visitors to New York go there just to shop. The biggest shops, selling all kinds of things, are Macy's and Bloomingdales. Tiffany's on Fifth Avenue sells beautiful jewellery but it is very expensive. Times Square and Broadway are the centre of the theatre area, and Greenwich Village has been the home of artists and musicians since the 1940s. There are many museums in New York and the biggest is the wonderful Metropolitan Museum of Art. Or if you get tired

A house in Savannah, Georgia

of the city, you can go into Central Park, a big area of green in the middle of the busy streets of Manhattan.

Washington DC is the capital of the USA. It was built in a special area, the District of Columbia (DC), on land that came from the states of Maryland and Virginia. It is different from most American cities because it has no skyscrapers; its highest building is the Capitol, home of the Senate and House of Representatives. You can visit the White House, where the President lives, as well as museums of history, art and air travel. Some of the city's most beautiful houses are in the old area of Georgetown.

Much further south are the old cities of Savannah, Georgia, and Charleston, South Carolina, where there are also many beautiful old houses. They look the same as they did 150 years ago or more. But not all southern cities are old. Atlanta in Georgia is big and modern, with one of the busiest airports in the world. There are plenty of jobs, and people think that it is a comfortable city to live in.

Away from the coast in the state of Illinois, Chicago is sometimes called the 'Windy City' because of the cold winds that blow in from Lake Michigan. The first really tall buildings were built in Chicago after the great fire of 1871. Today, the Sears Tower in Chicago (more than 500 metres high) is the tallest building in the USA. Frank Lloyd Wright (1867–1959), who made beautiful houses and other buildings, worked in Chicago and you can see examples of his houses there. Like any big city, Chicago has factories, shops, museums and restaurants, but only Chicago has Wrigley Field, the famous baseball field.

On the west coast, Seattle has become one of the most popular cities in America since the 1980s. In 1985 Starbucks started the fashion for Italian coffee shops here. In the 1990s

A casino in Las Vegas

it was the home of new music from bands like Pearl Jam and
Nirvana. Bill Gates of Microsoft, one of the richest men in
the world, was born in Seattle. Films and TV programmes
are made about people who live in Seattle. A city that was
once quiet has become crowded and more expensive.

Las Vegas in the hot, dry state of Nevada is full of casinos.
People win and lose thousands of dollars there, playing
cards or other games. People also go there to get married
quickly and easily. If you want, a man dressed like Elvis
Presley can be at your wedding!

14 California

More people live in California than in any other state – over 30 million of them. It is the biggest state after Texas and Alaska and it is a state of differences. The highest mountain in the USA outside Alaska is Mount Whitney in the east of the state; it is 4,420 metres high. And California has the lowest, driest place in the USA: Death Valley, which is 86 metres lower than the sea. It is very hot there (56.7°C on the hottest day, in 1913) and in some years it does not rain at all. But the north of the state is quite cold and wet. This is where

Redwood trees

San Francisco and Alcatraz

the great redwood trees grow – the tallest trees in the world. The biggest is 115.5 metres high. Also in the north is the Napa Valley area, where excellent wines are made. California grows more fruit and vegetables than any other state in the USA but it is also famous for its computer factories. Hewlett and Packard started their business in California, and Apple have their head offices there.

San Francisco is, many people think, one of the most beautiful cities in the world. In 1849, people came here to look for gold and they became known as 'Forty-Niners'. Jeans were first made in San Francisco by Levi Strauss in those days. The city grew fast but was nearly destroyed in 1906 by an earthquake and the fire which followed it. There was another big earthquake in 1989 when 62 people died, and everyone knows that one day there will be another. But 800,000 Americans continue living in San Francisco because life there is fun. San Francisco was the meeting place for two groups of people who wanted a life that was different from the life of ordinary people. In the 1950s there were the 'beatniks' (like writers Allen Ginsberg and Jack Kerouac), who wore black and were not interested in money and jobs. Then in the 1960s 'hippies' came to San Francisco. They wore bright clothes, had long hair, and wanted a world full of peace and love. 1967 was the 'summer of love', with songs that talked about peace and love and told young people, 'If you go to San Francisco, wear a flower in your hair'.

San Francisco is also famous for the Golden Gate Bridge, which was built in 1937 and joins the city to Marin County. More than 40 million journeys are made across it every year. It is 2.7 kilometres long and 67 metres above the water. From the bridge you can see the island of Alcatraz, which was a prison until 1963.

Los Angeles is the second biggest city in the USA, with 3.8 million people. It can take hours to drive from one side to the other – and people almost always drive! The number of cars means that the city has a problem with dirty air; in

The film world of Hollywood

some parts of the city crime is a problem too. But visitors still come to see places like Hollywood and Beverly Hills. The first film was made in Hollywood in 1911 in a place where orange trees used to grow. The first films, with actors like Rudolf Valentino, Charlie Chaplin, and Buster Keaton were silent, but then in 1927 films got sound. In the 1930s and 1940s famous stars like Clark Gable, Humphrey Bogart, and Katharine Hepburn appeared in films like *It Happened One Night*, *Casablanca*, and *The Philadelphia Story*. Some of the greatest films of the time came from the crime stories of the famous Californian writers Dashiell Hammett and Raymond Chandler. Chandler wrote about the detective Philip Marlowe, who was played by Bogart in *The Big Sleep*.

Today, films are big business – it costs millions of dollars to make them, but they can make millions of dollars more. On Hollywood Boulevard you can visit Mann's Chinese Theatre, where film stars have left the shapes of their hands and feet in the ground. You can visit Paramount Studios in Hollywood, where the *Godfather* films were made, or Universal Studios outside the city, where you can feel an earthquake or see King Kong and Jurassic Park. In Beverly Hills you can drive past the homes of famous stars.

Mickey Mouse first appeared in 1928 in films by Walt Disney. Disney died in 1966, but his company continues to make very popular films like *Pirates of the Caribbean*. Disneyland is the top place for tourists in California. It is in Orange County in the south of the state. If you visit Disneyland, you will meet Mickey Mouse and his friends walking around the park. You can visit the castle of Sleeping Beauty, ride on a river boat, or have an Indiana Jones or Tarzan adventure.

15 Beautiful places to visit

The USA has some of the biggest cities in the world, and more than three-quarters of its people live in cities or towns. This means that there are also some very empty places, which have not changed much since the first Europeans arrived. The government has kept some of them as national parks, beautiful natural places where people are not allowed to build houses or factories. Many artists have photographed the beautiful parks of America. One of the most famous is Ansel Adams, who was born in San Francisco a few years before the earthquake of 1906. Two of his favourite places

Mount Rainier

were Yosemite in northern California, which has been a park since 1890, and the coast of California.

Travelling north from California, you come to Oregon and then Washington. These states are cool and wet, but very beautiful, with big forests and high mountains. Here you will find a number of national parks like Mount Rainier and Crater Lake.

The wonderful Rocky Mountains are in the states of Wyoming, Montana, Colorado, Idaho and Utah, and are great for holidays. Walking, climbing, fishing, hunting, and horse-riding are some of the things visitors enjoy here. You can also enjoy winter sports in places like Aspen, where there is a lot of snow. The only big city in the Rockies is Denver. Also in the Rocky Mountains is Yellowstone Park in the states of Idaho, Wyoming, and Montana. It is famous for the geyser called Old Faithful that shoots hot water up into the air, up to 55 metres high. Salt Lake City, the capital city of Utah, is next to a lake that is much saltier than the sea. If you try to swim in this lake, you will find that you cannot stay under the water!

South of the Rockies is the hot, dry state of Arizona, where the land has fantastic colours: not just brown and green, but red, pink, orange, and blue. The most famous place in Arizona is the Grand Canyon. This deep river valley was made by the Colorado River cutting through the rock many thousands of years ago. Today it is 1,600 metres deep, 446 kilometres long, and between 0.4 and 24 kilometres wide with rocks in extraordinary shapes. You can walk down to the river, but it will take you two days to get there and back, and you must take plenty of water to drink.

Next to Arizona, New Mexico is another hot, dry state, where farming is difficult and the ordinary people are poor.

The Grand Canyon

Niagara Falls

But many artists have also come from other parts of America to live in and around Santa Fe and Taos. One of the first was Georgia O'Keeffe and there is a museum of her work in Santa Fe.

In the Badlands National Park of South Dakota visitors remember the Sioux who fought and died at Wounded Knee, but the Black Hills of Dakota are famous for Mount Rushmore, where the faces of four American presidents, Washington, Jefferson, Lincoln, and Theodore Roosevelt were cut in the rock. It took fourteen years, from 1927 to 1941. You can see them in the Hitchcock film *North by Northwest*, where Cary Grant nearly falls from the mountain while he is trying to escape.

Canada and the USA meet at the five Great Lakes, which are an important route for ships travelling from the Atlantic to the Midwest along the St Lawrence Seaway. The famous Niagara Falls are between Lakes Ontario and Erie. These waterfalls are 51

metres high. You can look at them from the top from Canada or the USA, or you can take a boat trip and see them from below. Together, Lakes Erie, Ontario, Huron, Michigan, and Superior cover 244,108 square kilometres – more than any other group of lakes in the world. If you go there in the summer, it is almost like going to the sea; you can lie on the beach or sail a boat. But in winter it is very cold.

Thousands of kilometres south of the Great Lakes is the state of Louisiana, which used to be French. The Mississippi River is 3,778 kilometres long and in the nineteenth century it was an important route between the North and the South. Mark Twain wrote wonderful stories about life on and around the river: *The Adventures of Tom Sawyer* (1876), and *Huckleberry Finn* (1884). Next to Louisiana, the state of Mississippi was also the home of several great writers like Tennessee Williams and William Faulkner.

Together the states of Maine, New Hampshire, Vermont, Massachusetts, Connecticut and Rhode Island are known as New England. Autumn, or 'fall' as the Americans call it, is a good time to visit New England, because the leaves on the trees turn yellow and orange and red and gold. October is a good month to see the colours at their best.

Autumn colours in New England

16 Hot and cold, big and small

Florida in the far Southeast is called the 'Sunshine State' because it is so warm and sunny. Oranges grow there, and visitors come to enjoy beach holidays. They can also visit Walt Disney World and the Kennedy Space Center. Florida has the Everglades, an area which is not like any other place in the USA. The land is very wet and has many trees, plants, animals and birds that are not found in other parts of America. But Florida is very popular with older people who want to live somewhere warm. This means new houses and roads, and building them has destroyed a lot of the land. There are also more and more factories, and some people are angry that this beautiful state is losing many of its wild birds and animals because of its dirty air and water.

Cold, lonely Alaska is the largest state in the USA, and Canada stands between it and the other states. Fishing and hunting used to bring money to Alaska, and gold was found there too. But today it is important for its oil. North America's highest mountain, Mount McKinley (6,194 metres), is in Alaska. A great way to travel there is by boat from Seattle. Most visitors go in summer; in winter it is very cold, and it is dark for most of the day because it is so far north. However, if you are lucky you will see the Northern Lights (aurora borealis), which fill the sky with fantastic colours.

Texas is the second biggest state after Alaska. There are

The Northern Lights

still cowboys who work there, but the modern state of Texas, like Alaska, is rich because of its oil. The smallest state of the USA is little Rhode Island to the east of Connecticut. Newport in Rhode Island has three big music festivals each year. In Texas the capital city, Austin, is also famous for its music. Janis Joplin sang there, as well as Bruce Springsteen, Van Morrison, and country singer Kinky Friedman, who also writes very funny crime books.

The holiday islands of Hawaii are a long way from the other states of the USA. Many Americans go there to enjoy the beaches, like the famous Waikiki Beach, and the warm sunshine. Although there are a lot of tourists, you can escape to quieter places where you can see trees, waterfalls and many unusual plants and birds. There are sadly only 9,000 true Hawaiians, but around a third of the people who live in the islands are part-Hawaiian.

But there are more interesting and exciting places to visit in the USA than will fit into one book. Choose what you prefer, busy city or quiet national park, cold mountains or warm sea, shopping or sports, and plan your own American journey!

Surfing in Hawaii

Canada
Washington
Montana
North Dakota
Minnesota
Vermont
Maine
Oregon
Idaho
Wyoming
South Dakota
Wisconsin
Michigan
New Hampshire
Boston
Massachusetts
Rhode Island
Connecticut
New York
Iowa
Chicago
Nebraska
Pennsylvania
New York
New Jersey
Nevada
Utah
Colorado
Illinois
Indiana
Ohio
Kansas
Missouri
West Virginia
Washington DC
Delaware
Maryland
Virginia
Kentucky
San Francisco
California
Arizona
New Mexico
Oklahoma
Arkansas
Tennessee
North Carolina
Atlantic Ocean
South Carolina
Mississippi
Alabama
Georgia
Texas
Pacific Ocean
Louisiana
New Orleans
N
Florida
Mexico
Alaska
Hawaii
0 km
300
600
900 km

GLOSSARY

alcohol strong drinks like wine, beer or whisky

area part of a town or country

artist a person who paints or draws pictures

celebrate to do something to show that you are happy because it is a special day

Christian following the teachings of Jesus Christ

colony a country or an area that is ruled by another country

corn a tall plant with big yellow seeds that you can eat

earthquake a sudden strong shaking of the ground

elect to choose somebody to be a leader by voting for them; **election** (*n*)

equal having the same rights as other people

freedom not being a slave; being able to do or say what you want

government a group of people who control a country; **govern** (*v*)

head the most important person in an organization

hunt to chase animals and kill them; **hunter** (*n*)

immigrant a person who comes to another country to live there

independent not controlled by another country; **independence** (*n*)

jewellery beautiful things that you wear on your ears, fingers, etc.

judge the person in court who decides how to punish somebody

law all the rules of a country; **break the law** to do something that the law does not allow; **pass a law** to make a new rule

museum a place where you can look at old or interesting things

oil a thick liquid from under the ground that we use for energy

ordinary not strange or special

particularly more than usual, or more than others

pie fruit cooked in a dish with pastry on the bottom

political party a group of people who have the same ideas about government

prejudice a strong idea that you do not like something, for a reason that is wrong or unfair

pumpkin a large round vegetable with a thick orange skin

record (*n & v*) a thin round piece of plastic that has music on it

religion believing in a god; **religious** (*adj*)

represent to speak for a group of people; **representative** (*n*)

right (*n*) what you are allowed to do by law; **civil rights** the right to vote, work, etc. equal to everybody else

separate away from other things or people

slave a person who belongs to another person and must work for them for no money

spicy having a strong taste and smell

state a part of a country with its own government

style a way of doing something

tax money that is paid to the government

tobacco leaves that are dried to make cigarettes

turkey a big bird that people keep on farms and that you can eat

vote to choose somebody in an election

war fighting between armies of different countries; **civil war** fighting between groups of people in the same country

waterfall a place where water falls from a high place to a low place

ACTIVITIES

Before Reading

1 Here are six famous places. Match the names with the photos.

1 ☐ Grand Canyon   4 ☐ Mount Rushmore

2 ☐ Hawaii   5 ☐ New York

3 ☐ Las Vegas   6 ☐ San Francisco

2 Which of these places would you most like to visit? Why?

ACTIVITIES

While Reading

Read Chapters 1 to 3. Are these sentences true (T) or false (F)? Rewrite the false sentences with the correct information.

1 The first Americans came from Asia.
2 There are more Hispanic people than Native Americans in the USA.
3 Pocahontas married John Smith.
4 The Pilgrim Fathers used slaves to farm the land.
5 Americans celebrate Thanksgiving in November.
6 Men in Boston threw boxes of tea into the sea because they wanted to drink coffee.
7 The chief of the American army was Thomas Jefferson.
8 The thirteen colonies became the first states of the USA.
9 The last state to join the United States of America was Utah.

Read Chapter 4. Choose the best question-words for these questions and then answer the questions.

What / Which / Who / Why

1 _____ did South Carolina decide to leave the United States?
2 _____ was the South's most famous soldier?
3 _____ farm boy from Kentucky became president?
4 _____ happened at Gettysburg in 1863?
5 _____ did John Wilkes Booth shoot President Lincoln?
6 _____ book tells the story of a rich Southern girl?

Read Chapters 5 and 6 and match these halves of sentences.

1 Farmers who came to live in the West . . .
2 When letters were carried by the Pony Express, they . . .
3 Many Native Americans either died of disease . . .
4 Without the buffalo . . .
5 After the Battle of Wounded Knee . . .
6 The Hopi and Zuni . . .

a) took ten days to cross the country.
b) Native Americans could not follow their usual way of life.
c) make beautiful jewellery.
d) or were killed in battle.
e) Native Americans had to live in 'reservations'.
f) grew food on their new farms.

Read Chapters 7 and 8 and answer these questions.

1 What happened to immigrants at Ellis Island?
2 Which large group of immigrants made their homes in the West?
3 Which language do most of today's immigrants speak?
4 Where did most black slaves use to work?
5 What was the 'Underground Railway'?
6 Before 1954, how were the lives of black people different in the South?
7 Why did Martin Luther King win the Nobel Peace Prize?
8 What did Hurricane Katrina do in 2005?

Read Chapters 9 to 11 and complete these sentences with the correct words.

1 In the USA *the President / Congress* makes the laws.
2 The longest time that anybody can be president is *four / eight* years.
3 The Republican Party is more popular in the *South / North* of the USA.
4 The presidents from the Bush family are *father and son / brothers.*
5 In *40 / 60* per cent of American families, the husband and wife both work.
6 To Americans, the date 'nine eleven' means *11 September / 9 November.*
7 Most Americans *walk / drive* to work.
8 The most popular sport in America is *football / baseball.*
9 California is famous for its *wine / coffee.*
10 Corn bread belongs to the style of food called *Cajun / soul* food.

Read Chapter 12. Match the music with the places.

1 blues   a) Nashville
2 soul   b) New Orleans
3 jazz   c) Mississippi
4 country   d) New York
5 rap   e) Detroit

Read Chapters 13 and 14. Then choose the correct words to complete the sentences.

Alcatraz, Boston, Cambridge, Chicago, Death Valley, Disneyland, Hollywood, Las Vegas, New York, Washington DC

1 Harvard opened in _____ in 1636.
2 _____ was the home of the Kennedy family.
3 Central Park is a green place in the centre of _____.
4 The president lives in _____.
5 _____ is called the 'Windy City'.
6 People go to _____ to win – or lose – lots of money.
7 Nowhere in the USA is lower than _____.
8 _____ used to be a prison.
9 _____ is the film capital of the USA.
10 The most popular place for tourists in California is _____.

Read Chapters 15 and 16. Here are some untrue sentences. Change them into true sentences.

1 Ansel Adams wrote books about the national parks of the USA.
2 Oregon and Washington have hot, dry weather.
3 Old Faithful is in Denver.
4 The Grand Canyon is 1,600 metres long.
5 Mount Rushmore is in Arizona.
6 The Great Lakes lie between the USA and Mexico.
7 Tom Sawyer wrote about life on the Mississippi River.
8 Most people visit Alaska in the winter.
9 Texas is rich because of its forests.
10 Hawaii is famous for its supermarkets.

ACTIVITIES

After Reading

1 **Match the people with the sentences. Then use the sentences to write a short description of each person. Use pronouns (*he, she*) and linking words (*and, because, but, then, who*).**

Johnny Cash / Martin Luther King / Pocahontas / General Sherman / Harriet Tubman / George Washington

1 _____ was the daughter of a Native American chief.

2 _____ was known as 'The Man in Black'.

3 _____ fought for the civil rights of black people.

4 _____ was a slave.

5 _____ fought for the North in the Civil War.

6 _____ was a rich farmer from Virginia.

7 _____ took his soldiers from Atlanta to the sea.

8 _____ escaped from slavery in 1849.

9 _____ helped the English people in Jamestown.

10 _____ became the leader of the US army after the Civil War.

11 _____ was a famous country singer.

12 _____ became the first President of the USA.

13 _____ helped other slaves to escape from the South.

14 _____ won the Nobel Peace Prize.

15 _____ later went to England with her husband, John Rolfe.

16 _____ went back to his farm in 1797.

17 _____ sold millions of records.

18 _____ was killed in Memphis in 1968.

2 Find these words in the box below and draw lines through them. The words go from left to right and from top to bottom.

alcohol, area, colony, corn, elect, equal, hunt, immigrant, judge, law, museum, oil, right, separate, slave, spicy, state, tax, tobacco, turkey

G	O	C	V	E	Q	U	A	L	E	R
N	J	O	M	L	A	W	E	N	T	I
T	U	R	K	E	Y	O	M	F	S	M
O	D	N	T	C	S	H	U	N	T	M
B	G	H	A	T	P	E	S	P	A	I
A	E	E	L	O	I	P	E	L	T	G
C	E	B	C	Y	C	T	U	H	E	R
C	O	L	O	N	Y	E	M	P	E	A
O	I	O	H	P	L	A	E	F	O	N
R	L	T	O	H	E	R	I	G	H	T
P	E	S	L	A	V	E	O	T	A	X
P	S	E	P	A	R	A	T	E	L	E

Now write down all the letters that do not have lines through them, beginning with the first line and going across each line to the end. You should have 44 letters which make a sentence of 10 words.

1 What is the sentence?
2 Who said it, and where?
3 What had just happened?

3 Choose a place in the USA and write an e-mail to a friend
   about it.

From:
Subject:

Hi_____!

How are you? I'm having a wonderful time in _____.
Yesterday we went to _____ and we saw
_____. That was great, but the most exciting thing
was _____. Today we're going to _____.
That's in _____. I hope I'll be able to _____.
I'll tell you all about it in my next e-mail.

Bye, _____

---

4 Now choose a place in the USA that you would like to visit –
   a city, a state, a national park, or perhaps a place like Niagara
   Falls or Mount Rushmore. Find out more information about
   it, then make a poster or give a talk about it to your class.
   Find answers to these questions:

What do you know about the history of the place?

What can visitors see and do there?

What is different or special about it?

Is there a famous food, kind of music, person, or building
   that you can find in this place?

Why would you like to go there?

ABOUT THE AUTHOR

Alison Baxter was a teacher of English for ten years. Her first teaching job was in Quebec, and she then went on to teach in Spain, Jordan, and the South Pacific. Then she became an editor of English language books, including the Oxford Bookworms series.

While Alison lived in Quebec, she travelled a lot in North America and she has happy memories of many of the places in this book. Her most exciting trip began in the Rocky Mountain National Park, one of the most beautiful places she has ever seen. From Denver, Alison and a friend took a bus to Arizona through the desert to see the Grand Canyon, which they saw from a little plane. It was magnificent but quite frightening because when the plane took off it went down, not up! Then they went to Los Angeles and to San Francisco – Alison's favourite American city. From there Alison drove up through northern California and Oregon to Seattle, stopping to look at the giant redwood trees. Then she returned to Quebec on the train that crosses Canada from Vancouver to Montreal.

Alison was born in Oxford and now she enjoys living there again. She is the chief executive of an Oxfordshire charity. In her spare time she likes to garden, cook, and practise yoga.

OXFORD BOOKWORMS LIBRARY

Classics • Crime & Mystery • Factfiles • Fantasy & Horror
Human Interest • Playscripts • Thriller & Adventure
True Stories • World Stories

The OXFORD BOOKWORMS LIBRARY provides enjoyable reading in English, with a wide range of classic and modern fiction, non-fiction, and plays. It includes original and adapted texts in seven carefully graded language stages, which take learners from beginner to advanced level. An overview is given on the next pages.

All Stage 1 titles are available as audio recordings, as well as over eighty other titles from Starter to Stage 6. All Starters and many titles at Stages 1 to 4 are specially recommended for younger learners. Every Bookworm is illustrated, and Starters and Factfiles have full-colour illustrations.

The OXFORD BOOKWORMS LIBRARY also offers extensive support. Each book contains an introduction to the story, notes about the author, a glossary, and activities. Additional resources include tests and worksheets, and answers for these and for the activities in the books. There is advice on running a class library, using audio recordings, and the many ways of using Oxford Bookworms in reading programmes. Resource materials are available on the website <www.oup.com/elt/gradedreaders>.

The *Oxford Bookworms Collection* is a series for advanced learners. It consists of volumes of short stories by well-known authors, both classic and modern. Texts are not abridged or adapted in any way, but carefully selected to be accessible to the advanced student.

You can find details and a full list of titles in the *Oxford Bookworms Library Catalogue* and *Oxford English Language Teaching Catalogues*, and on the website <www.oup.com/elt/gradedreaders>.

THE OXFORD BOOKWORMS LIBRARY
GRADING AND SAMPLE EXTRACTS

STARTER • 250 HEADWORDS

present simple – present continuous – imperative –
can/cannot, must – *going to* (future) – simple gerunds ...

Her phone is ringing – but where is it?

Sally gets out of bed and looks in her bag. No phone. She looks under the bed. No phone. Then she looks behind the door. There is her phone. Sally picks up her phone and answers it. *Sally's Phone*

STAGE 1 • 400 HEADWORDS

... past simple – coordination with *and, but, or* –
subordination with *before, after, when, because, so* ...

I knew him in Persia. He was a famous builder and I worked with him there. For a time I was his friend, but not for long. When he came to Paris, I came after him – I wanted to watch him. He was a very clever, very dangerous man. *The Phantom of the Opera*

STAGE 2 • 700 HEADWORDS

... present perfect – *will* (future) – *(don't) have to, must not, could* –
comparison of adjectives – simple *if* clauses – past continuous –
tag questions – *ask/tell* + infinitive ...

While I was writing these words in my diary, I decided what to do. I must try to escape. I shall try to get down the wall outside. The window is high above the ground, but I have to try. I shall take some of the gold with me – if I escape, perhaps it will be helpful later. *Dracula*

STAGE 3 • 1000 HEADWORDS

... *should, may* – present perfect continuous – *used to* – past perfect –
causative – relative clauses – indirect statements ...

Of course, it was most important that no one should see
Colin, Mary, or Dickon entering the secret garden. So Colin
gave orders to the gardeners that they must all keep away
from that part of the garden in future. *The Secret Garden*

STAGE 4 • 1400 HEADWORDS

... past perfect continuous – passive (simple forms) –
would conditional clauses – indirect questions –
relatives with *where/when* – gerunds after prepositions/phrases ...

I was glad. Now Hyde could not show his face to the world
again. If he did, every honest man in London would be proud
to report him to the police. *Dr Jekyll and Mr Hyde*

STAGE 5 • 1800 HEADWORDS

... future continuous – future perfect –
passive (modals, continuous forms) –
would have conditional clauses – modals + perfect infinitive ...

If he had spoken Estella's name, I would have hit him. I was so
angry with him, and so depressed about my future, that I could
not eat the breakfast. Instead I went straight to the old house.
Great Expectations

STAGE 6 • 2500 HEADWORDS

... passive (infinitives, gerunds) – advanced modal meanings –
clauses of concession, condition

When I stepped up to the piano, I was confident. It was as if I
knew that the prodigy side of me really did exist. And when I
started to play, I was so caught up in how lovely I looked that
I didn't worry how I would sound. *The Joy Luck Club*

BOOKWORMS · FACTFILES · STAGE 3
Martin Luther King

ALAN C. McLEAN

The United States in the 1950s and 60s was a troubled place. Black people were angry, because they did not have the same rights as whites. It was a time of angry words, of marches, of protests, a time of bombs and killings.

But above the angry noise came the voice of one man – a man of peace. 'I have a dream,' said Martin Luther King, and it was a dream of blacks and whites living together in peace and freedom. This is the story of an extraordinary man, who changed American history in his short life.

BOOKWORMS · FACTFILES · STAGE 3
Australia and New Zealand

CHRISTINE LINDOP

What do you find in these two countries at the end of the world? One is an enormous island, where only twenty million people live – and the other is two long, narrow islands, with ten sheep for every person. One country has the biggest rock in all the world, and a town where everybody lives under the ground; the other has a beach where you can sit beside the sea in a pool of hot water, and lakes that are bright yellow, green, and blue. Open this book and start your journey – to two countries where something strange, beautiful, or surprising waits around every corner.